When
the
Bamboo
Bends

When the Bamboo Bends

Christ and Culture in Japan

MASAO TAKENAKA

Risk
BOOK SERIES

WCC Publications, Geneva

Cover design: Rob Lucas
Cover illustration: Masao Takenaka

ISBN 2-8254-1362-3

© 2002, WCC Publications
World Council of Churches
150 route de Ferney, P.O. Box 2100
1211 Geneva 2, Switzerland

Web site: http//www.wcc-coe.org

No. 100 in the Risk Book Series

Printed in Switzerland

Table of Contents

Bamboo grove, Kyoto

Clean wind gradually comes

Preface

This book is intended to be a companion to my earlier book *God Is Rice*, which was published in 1986 by the World Council of Churches as part of its Risk Series. This book caught the attention of a large number of readers and went on to be reprinted several times. Rather than revising that edition, I decided to write a new book, this time focusing on a new image – that of bamboo.

Like rice, bamboo is a common and greatly appreciated plant, found in many parts of Asia. It can be planted in a garden to catch a breeze, and used for a variety of domestic purposes – constructing houses, making water pipes, fences, various household implements and furniture. It can also be used for scaffolding. Bamboo is used in cultural contexts such as dance and drama and festivals throughout Asia (e.g. in house decorations at new year). We enjoy the music of bamboo flutes and the rhythm of the bamboo dance (where canes of bamboo are used). In the traditional Japanese tea ceremony and Noh drama bamboo is also used in various ways; flower baskets and spoons.

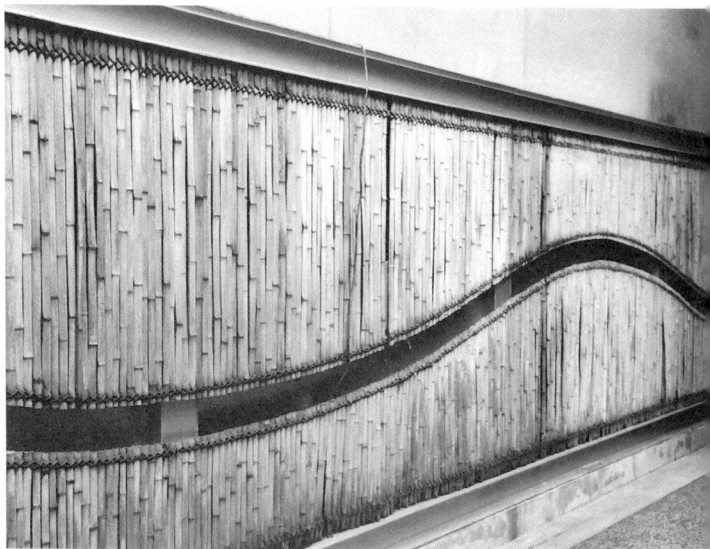

Bamboo fence

It is hard to imagine Asian culture deprived of bamboo. Its popularity is well attested by the postage stamps of various Asian countries. There are stamps showing pandas eating bamboo leaves. In Thailand and Singapore, bamboo forms the background of stamps depicting local birds and butterflies. In Korea, a bamboo flute is depicted on a stamp.

Asian stamps featuring bamboo

In Japan, too, the image of bamboo appears on official stamps. One of Ukiyoe's prints, depicting a scene of daily life in Japan, has frequently been used on stamps; it shows both a bamboo fence and an umbrella made with bamboo stems. Another stamp was graced by one of Heihachiro Fukuda's refined painting of bamboo shoots.

In Japan there is a well-known folk-tale called *Taketori Monogatari* in which a girl is found in a bamboo grove and grows up to become a beautiful princess. She ultimately

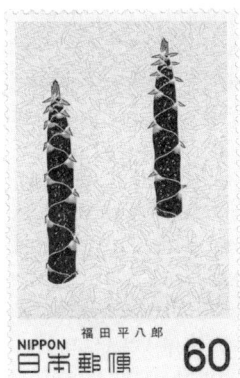

returns to heaven in spite of the admiration of many young men. Scenes from Noh drama, using scenery made out of bamboo, have also been shown on stamps.

As well as having a whole host of practical uses bamboo is also imbued with deep spiritual meaning, especially in northeast Asia – China, Korea and Japan. The purpose of this book is to reflect on the implications the spiritual meaning bamboo has for our earthly life in the light of Christian faith.

As it spread and developed in the West, Christianity adapted to Western culture. An intimate relationship developed between the Christian faith and such Western symbols as bread, grapes and sheep, which are used to convey significant parts of the Christian message. The Japanese, however, had never seen bread until Portuguese traders and missionaries brought it to Japan in the 16th century. In Japan bread is still called *pan*, the Portuguese term. Sheep, too, are not native to Japanese culture: I have only ever seen them in zoos. Bread and sheep are foreign, not naturally a part of ordinary Japanese life.

I believe that the Christian gospel has universal implications based on the revelation of Jesus Christ. I believe that culture is not only a gift from God but also the basis of people's identity. Christianity, then, is universal while culture is local. In this sense, it is highly significant to consider the relationship between Christian faith and the role of bamboo in cultural expression in Japan. Following the introductory chapters, I will depict four aspects of bamboo and their spiritual symbolism. Firstly, that the bamboo grove invites a clean wind; secondly, that it bends and is flexible. Thirdly, bamboo roots stretch in solidarity, and lastly, the hollow, empty stem of the bamboo. I have tried in each case to lead the discussion from the biological characteristics of bamboo into their cultural and religious significance. Asian religions, especially Buddhism, have long considered bamboo as a "companion" or "friend". Thus, reflecting on bamboo naturally promotes dialogue with other religions.

This is not intended to be a systematic treatment of the subject. It does not follow the style of Calvin's *Institutes* but rather the informal reflection of Luther's *Table Talk*. I have included various illustrations and I would like to express my gratitude to all those who contributed their art to this book. Their creative support has made this book more enjoyable and meaningful. In appreciation there is a list of acknowledgments at the end, together with a brief bibliography, for those who want make further study of the subject.

The original lecture on which this book is based was delivered in January 2001 at Seiwa College, as a memorial lecture to commemorate my teaching service there after retiring from Doshisha University. I would like to express my gratitude to President Mitsuo Miyata and the members of the faculty and the staff of Seiwa College who invited me to work there and to give this lecture. I would especially like to express my appreciation to Dr Hata Okamura, a notable biologist, who was my colleague at Seiwa and who provided me with valuable insights. She is the author of the monumental book, *Illustrated Horticultural Bamboo Species*. I would also like to express my thanks to the students who attended my lecture. Their careful attention and thoughtful responses encouraged me. I also presented a condensed version of this lecture at a research seminar at the Institute of Humanities and Social Sciences at Doshisha University in April 2001. I owe thanks to the members of the institute. They stimulated my thoughts as we engaged in a joint study of Christianity and social problems in modern Japan. Finally, I would like to express gratitude to my wife, Fumiko, who passed away three years ago after the companionship of 47 years of married life. She would have enjoyed this book since she also shared an appreciation of the gift of bamboo. It is my sincere hope that this humble attempt will encourage others, in different parts of the world, to think about the relationship between Christ and their own local cultures.

1. Bamboo as a Symbol

With more than 40 genuses and 600 kinds, bamboo is one of the most common and widely spread plants in Asia. Tenshin Okakura (1862-1913) (art curator and author of *The Book of Tea*, 1904) once said that "Asia is one". But at the same time he also noted that Asia is characterized by a diverse history, many cultures, a great variety of religions, and that conflict and domination exist between nations within Asia.

In spite of the differences, it is still safe to say that there are many things in common between the countries of Asia. One is the habit of eating rice. There may be many varieties of rice and methods of preparing it, but everyone loves to eat rice. We can all gladly pray, "Give us this day our daily rice" instead of "our daily bread". Bamboo is well appreciated throughout Asia. It has many applications in everyday life and penetrates many areas of Asian culture. Another commonality is the monsoon season. To different degrees, many parts of Asia experience a monsoon climate with its characteristic seasonal wind and rain patterns. This weather plays a vital role in the cultivation of rice and of bamboo.

Biologically, bamboo is a member of the rice family. The two, then, are intimately related to one another. In *God Is Rice*, I considered the meaning of the Christian faith in Asia through the use, importance and symbolism of rice. This time I would like to study the bamboo, since it is so commonly found throughout Asia and so strongly rooted in Asian culture. My name is Takenaka Masao, which literally means Bamboo Centre Right Husband. My wife's maiden name was Hayashi, which means Wood. We were practically a bamboo family!

Many foreigners visiting Asia notice the widespread use of bamboo in the material culture of many communities. Bamboo is everywhere. Many houses are surrounded and protected by bamboo fences. We seldom plant a garden without bamboo. An old saying runs, "Even if we do not have beef in the meal, we should have bamboo in the home." While without beef we may lack nourishment, without bamboo in the home, we lose spirituality.

◁ *Sofu-an, tea house at Kobe College*

Bamboo fence, Sagano, Kyoto

*Bamboo fountain,
Kansai Seminar
House, Kyoto*

After we have entered a house through its bamboo gate, we find that bamboo is used all around: in the ceilings, walls and floors, as well as in more decorative items such as flower vases, kettle stands and pillars. Bamboo has also been long used for making utensils such as spoons, knives, chopsticks, baskets, plates, water bottles, brooms, rakes and sandals, to name a few everyday household items.

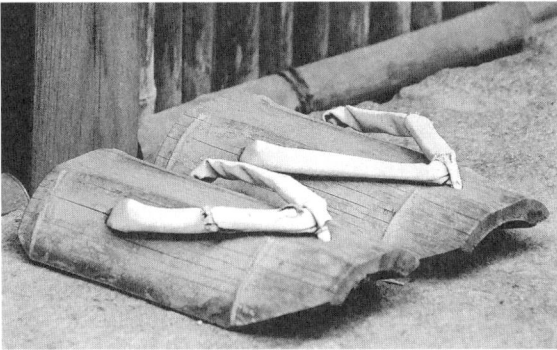

Bamboo sandals

Bamboo Thicket *from the* Hiroshima Panels *by Iri and Toshi Maruki*

A poem, also entitled *Bamboo Thicket,* runs:

Nowhere could people find shelter
except in the bamboo thickets of the suburbs.

"This is not an earthquake."
"What is it then?"
"A ball of flame bombs?"
"A new type probably."
"No, it's a death-ray, I'm sure."
"There was a flash and a bang."
"No, we didn't hear a bang."
"It was so dazzling. It was 'Pika'."
"When it struck me..."

Lots of things to talk about
in the bamboo thickets in the suburbs.

Many wounded people were carried into
the bamboo thickets and they found that
each bamboo stem was also burnt
on the side facing
the centre of the explosion.
The wind rustled through the bamboo thickets
and the wounded groaned.
Then cries for help were heard
but none had the courage or strength
to go to their aid
and a field hospital in a private home
was too crowded to admit any more.

A human figure under the Mataki Bridge
whose age or sex no one could tell
bowing its head low, was found dead
on the morning of August 26, 1945.
It had survived for twenty days
since the instant of the fatal explosion.
No one moved the corpse
until a typhoon-flood in September
washed it away into the sea.

The bamboo thickets provided refuge at the time of the Hiroshima disaster. It is also said that during an earthquake a bamboo thicket will afford great protection.

At the top of the hill of Otokoyama Hachiman, south of Kyoto, which is surrounded by rich bamboo groves, there is a special memorial to Thomas Edison (1847-1931) who is famous for inventing the incandescent light bulb with a carbon filament. After countless trials he succeeded by using bamboo for the filament. The monument was constructed in 1929 to commemorate the 50th anniversary of the invention of the electric lamp by Edison. To the left of the monument the following words of Edison are carved:

Genius is one per cent inspiration
And ninety-nine per cent perspiration

Bamboo not only provides physical comfort and convenient tools but also it gives a foundation for cultural expression. Bamboo features in the tale of *Taketori Monogatari*, the story of Kaguyahime, a beautiful princess born in a bamboo bush. In another well known ancient tale seven wise men enjoy a delightful dialogue as they search for their way through a bamboo thicket. Just as in ancient Greece, where philosophers used dialogue in their search for truth, the seven Oriental sages in the bamboo thicket have become a model, in northeast Asia, for discussion which aims to seek out the truth.

The usefulness and cleanness of bamboo have made it a popular material for use in various traditional Japanese cultural contexts. In music, a bamboo flute, called a *shaku hachi*, is ideal for expressing soft, tender melodies. In Indonesia, a musical instrument called an *anklung*, which also produces very gentle and expressive music, is made from bamboo.

The use of bamboo in tea ceremonies is also worth noting. Participants traditionally enter a garden through a tiny gate which is usually made of bamboo and which forms a demarcation between secular and spiritual space. The tea house, which is a place of communion and appreciation, employs bamboo materials which help promote an atmosphere and spirit of simplicity and purity. A number of the basic tools of the tea ceremony are made out of bamboo: the

6

chashaku (teaspoon), the *chasen* (whisk), the *hanaike* (flower basket) and the *hishaku* (ladle). Other items such as the *futaoki* (base for the lid to rest on), the *kamashiki* (kettle-rest), the *kogo* (incense case), and the *hashi* (chopsticks) are frequently made of bamboo. Some of these items are the products of elaborate processes but in general it is true to say that bamboo is used extensively because it is widely available, easily worked and makes beautifully simple utensils.

Noh theatre screen, Kansai Seminar House, Kyoto

In traditional Noh drama the image of the pine tree occupies the centre of the backdrop, and bamboo is found on the right side of the stage. As the actors approach the stage from the *hashigakari*, (a bridge leading on to the stage), the first thing they see is this image of bamboo, which is meant to reinforce in them a spirit of faithfulness and purity as they begin their performance.

The pine, plum and bamboo are symbols of celebration in Japan. At new year, every family decorates the front of their house with pine and bamboo to seek blessings for the coming year. In northeast Asia each of the four seasons is represented by a plant: the orchid for spring, bamboo for summer, chrysanthemum for autumn and plum for winter. In Japan there is much emphasis placed on expressing one's feelings about the seasons. In many traditional Japanese poems, such as the 31-syllable *waka* and the 17-syllable *haiku,* a reference to a season is included and these poems are used as seasonal greetings.

At his acceptance speech for the Nobel Prize for Literature in 1968, Yasunari Kawabata quoted a poem by Dogen (1200–53):

> In the spring, cherry blossoms,
> In the summer the cuckoo,
> In autumn the moon, and
> In winter the snow, clear, cold.

Speaking of the plum in winter, Joseph Hardy Neeshima (1843–90), founder of Doshisha University, appreciating the bursting buds on the plum tree in the winter, said:

> Truth is just like the winter plum blossom
> It dares to bloom despite snow and wind.

Neeshima had been a restless youth deeply unsatisfied with the conformity and restrictions of traditional Japanese society. Where he grew up, everything was strictly defined by the lord of his clan, to whom, by tradition, he owed absolute fealty. In 1864, he secretly stowed away on an American ship and travelled to the United States. At that time Japan's national policy of isolationism banned citizens of Japan from travelling abroad. Neeshima completed his studies in the United States and, in 1875, returned to Kyoto, the old capital city of Japan, to establish Doshisha, a Christian school. It was a difficult project; almost impossible. As one observer remarked, "To establish a Christian school in a conservative traditional city is just like commanding Mount Hiei

Truth is like a winter plum blossom, *painting in* sumi *by Masao Takenaka*

to jump into Lake Biwa." Neeshima wrote his plum blossom poem at the time of the year when the trees have shed all their leaves. But he saw a bud on the branch of a plum tree – a foretaste of the spring to come. It gave him hope that something was happening despite the snow and wind.

We can distinguish between two kinds of knowledge. One is rational knowledge, at which we arrive through reasoning and argument. The other is a gradual awakening to reality. Rational argument can be termed *yah-yah* knowledge; the other, which comes through encounters with the reality and beauty of everyday life can be called *ha-hah* knowledge.

We can find a *ha-hah* experience in the book of Jeremiah. Jeremiah was called to be a prophet among the nations. He knew that he would not be able to perform the task. "I am only a youth," he said. Then, the word of the Lord came to him, saying, "Jeremiah, what do you see?" He said, "I see a branch of an almond tree" (Jer. 1:11). The Hebrew words for almond also means "to awaken". Now, the almond blooms early February and is a sign that spring is on the way. At a deeper level the story is an allegory for the awakening of people to the living reality of God's presence – a Biblical *ha-hah* experience.

To return to bamboo, we can see that the family seal of the Neeshima family contains the *sasa*, a kind of bamboo. When Neeshima was a boy he was severely punished by his grandfather when he failed to obey his mother's commands. He was locked in a closet for an hour and he kept on crying even after he was released. His grandfather said, "Do not cry", and told him the story of bamboo. "I do not beat the bamboo grass because I do not like it." He said that you beat the bamboo in winter to knock off the snow covering the young shoots. You should grow steadily, as the bamboo does even when bending under the weight of snow. Neeshima learned an important lesson,

新島家の家紋

The Neeshima family seal

namely, that one must grow with patience, bearing one's burdens, just as bamboo never gives up while being bent by snow and by wind. So we will continue the journey to discover the full symbolism and meaning of bamboo in the light of Christian faith.

Bamboo Madonna, *Sadao Watanabe*

2. Bamboo in a Christian Context

We have acknowledged the popular use of bamboo in various aspects of the life of Asian peoples. Here we would like to see how Asian Christians have used bamboo in expressing their Christian faith.

Dambanang Kawayan (Fishermen's Chapel), the Philippines

In the Philippines there are many examples of the use of bamboo in the life and mission of the church. There is a fishermen's chapel (Dambanang Kawayan) near the capital, Manila where the ceiling, altar floor and altar furniture is almost entirely made of bamboo. It is often called a bamboo church. This Roman Catholic church was designed by Fr Ben Villiote and built in 1968.

Carlos Francisco (1912-69) was a distinguished 20th-century artist in the Philippines. He worked closely with rural communities in the Philippines and depicted the "bamboo dance" in one of his paintings of local festivals. In a work titled *The Madonna of Bamboo*, he placed Mary and Jesus against a background of bamboo. The painting reflects the message of the incarnation in a Philippines context.

The first Asian Christian women artists consultation was held in Hong Kong in September 1992. Its theme was

The Madonna of Bamboo *by Carlos V. Francisco*

Pista sa Nayon (Bamboo Dance) *by Carlos V. Francisco*

"Creation and Spirituality: Asian Women Expressing Christian Faith". Brenda V. Fajardo, who is active among women artists in the Philippines, presented a work entitled *Creation*. In this work the central area is a vortex whose middle is the source of all energy – the spirit of Christ symbolized by a lotus, striking in red and gold. A man and a woman appear in the middle of a stand of bamboo symbolizing the Creation. Panels depicting the historic struggle of the women of the Philippines surround the centre. The use of bamboo in the painting is effective both as a natural element in the Philippines and as a representation of the spirit and courage of the country's women.

In the work of Chen Yuandu in China in the early part of the 20th century we find an example of classical Christian art. Archbishop Celso Constantini, the first apostolic nuncio to China and a great art connoisseur, encouraged Chen to express the biblical story in traditional Chinese style. Later on, Chen was baptized and became known as Luke Chen. Luke Chen worked as a teacher of traditional Chinese painting at the Catholic Furen University in Beijing and trained a successor. During the Cultural Revolution, the painting class was discontinued. Today artists, such as Mali and Wo Ye in Shanghai, once again continue the tradition and style of Luke Chen's work.

Jesus and Children *by Luke Chen*

Holy Mother and Son *by Mali and Wo Ye*

In China today Protestant churches place a strong emphasis on expressing Christian faith through art done in Chinese style. At the Nanjing Theological Seminary a course on Christian art is compulsory for all seminarians. Also in Nanjing, the Amity Christian Art Centre coordinates the work of Christian artists and encourages the promotion of art throughout the provinces. This initiative is supported by national leaders such as Han Wenzao, the president of the China Christian Council and secretary general of the Amity Foundation. He says, "We Chinese Christians lay great emphasis on our national artistic forms when we promote Christian art work in China. We make such emphasis in order to do away with the concept of it as an 'imported religion' and to spread the good news on Chinese soil."

Bamboo Rooted in the Rock *by Bao Guping*

Bao Guping acknowledges the strength of bamboo in his painting *Bamboo Rooted in the Rock*. The accompanying calligraphy is a poem in which he tries to convey the message of bamboo, whose roots are firmly planted beside the rock even though its fine branches are being bent by the wind. Traditional Chinese painting, influenced by Taoist philosophy, usually uses landscapes to express the power and spirit of nature. Quite often Christian artists who work in this traditional style include a poem or text to express the Christian message. In this way they profess the Christian faith while working in traditional Chinese style.

Christianity came to Japan in 1549 with the missionary Francisco Xavier (1506–52). It had a promising beginning and was even encouraged by the national leader, Nobunaga. Soon, however, its followers suffered severe persecution (started by Hideyoshi) and in 1614 Christianity was prohibited throughout the country. Persecution was extensive and so severe that many Christians were forced to renounce their faith. Some where even martyred. This persecution continued for round 260 years. The ban was officially lifted in 1873. During this time Christianity went underground and followers were known as Crypto-Christians. There are a

Cross and Maria-Kannon engraved on bamboo,
Ikenaga Collection at Kobe City Museum, Japan

number of common items which Crypto-Christians used to strengthen their inner faith in Jesus Christ.

Among these items, there are bamboo hangings on which the Cross and Maria-Kannon (Mary-Goddess of Mercy) were engraved. Crypto-Christians used such objects to honour Christ and to secretly sustain their faith. It is significant that bamboo was used for such purposes. Bamboo was and still is widely available, true, but its use also deepens the meaning of artefacts and images as bamboo also symbolizes faithfulness and loyalty.

Sadao Watanabe, one of the best-known Japanese Christian artists, produced a work called "Kakure (Crypto)-Christian". In it, we see two Maria-Kannons, one of whom is wearing a *kimono* with a design of bamboo on it. In another work, entitled *Mother and Child* he again shows Mary dressed in a *kimono* with a design of bamboo leaves on it (p.10).

So we can see that the use of bamboo in Asia has not been limited to practical household utensils; it has also been

Two Maria-Kannons *by Sadao Watanabe, 1984*

widely used in various traditional cultural contexts. Furthermore, we have learned how bamboo has been used in the life and mission of Asian churches. It will be good to continue exploring the meaning of bamboo in the light of Christian faith. But before that, we should critically appraise the relationship between Christianity and culture in Japan.

3. Christianity in Japan Today

Up to now we have been concentrating on the positive attributes of bamboo. My guru, H. Richard Niebuhr, professor of Christian ethics at Yale University, would suddenly remark, in the midst of complex discussions, "Wait a moment! What's going on?" During endless debates about good and bad he would recast the issue in terms of what God was doing there. The Bible does not mention bamboo, nor does Jesus speak of it. Yet we can appreciate God in and through bamboo. We need to reflect both appreciatively and critically on what God is doing through bamboo. Bamboo, is a part of God's creation; it is one of God's gifts.

Jesus blessed the nameless flowers of the field and remarked that "even Solomon in all his glory was not arrayed like one of these" (Matt. 16:29); likewise he would surely have reminded us of the lively spirit embodied in the bamboo in our fields. This is not nature worship, not natural theology, but a theology of nature based on biblical revelation. Today, having so greatly damaged our natural environment, we should start advocating acceptance of nature as a gift of God and assume responsibility for stewardship of the planet rather than domination over it (Gen. 2:15).

At the end of the second world war, while a student at the school of economics at Kyoto University, I was drafted for military service. At this time, I had to face some of the less palatable uses of bamboo. I was drafted into the regular army at a time when, because of a steel shortage, bayonet covers had begun to be made of bamboo. Bamboo was also widely used as a weapon for killing the enemy. We should remember this example in our critical assessment of bamboo and its Christian symbolism.

In Japan today the content of textbooks is widely debated. The government wants schools to have the freedom to choose between a variety of textbooks and not force them to accept one standard set of texts. Some interest groups, however, want all modern history textbooks to include a justification for Japanese expansionist policy. They also want to exclude critical analysis of the issue. However, from my perspective rigorous critical assessment of Japan's history is vital, in order to both understand the past and stimulate continued interest in history and its lessons.

In his book called *The Kingdom of God in America* (1937), H. Richard Niebuhr put forth three hypotheses for analyzing American Christianity in terms of the kingdom of God. Firstly, that the Kingdom of God has been the dominant idea throughout American Christianity but that it has not always had a consistent meaning (he examines this diversified notion of the kingdom of God). Secondly, that it is a dialectical concept (embracing both human depravity and offering redeeming love). And thirdly, that American Christianity should be seen in the light of its faith in a living, sovereign and transforming God. These three convictions can be applied wherever one is examining the relationship between Christianity and culture. In his last book, *Radical Monotheism and Western Culture* (1960), Niebuhr extended his basic approach and convictions to analyze Western culture in the light of radical monotheism. It will be interesting to undertake a similar analysis of Japanese culture.

Christianity in Japan exists in the midst of religious pluralism. Religious life in Japan is pluralistic and ambiguous. It is pluralistic because a number of religions co-exist within society and often even within an individual. It is ambiguous because a person's religious commitment may not be absolutely fixed. As a result, he or she may well shift religions according to circumstances. Looking at religious statistics for Japan, one is immediately struck by the extent of this religious diversity.

Although the population of Japan is around 120 million, the statistics show that there is nearly twice that number of religious practitioners. These statistics were compiled by the Japanese ministry of cultural affairs on the basis of reports filed by national religious organizations. Assuming the figures are reliable, how can such strange results be interpreted?

Religious statistics in Japan in 2000

Religion	Place of Worship						Teachers		Believers
	Shrines	Temples	Churches	Preaching Centres	Others	Total	Males (Foreigners)	Females (Foreigmers)	
Shintoism	81,261	19	6065	1221	844	89,410	52,812 (57)	27,590 (58)	106,241,598
Buddhism	13	77,097	2634	2582	4334	86,660	134,291 (150)	81,780 (110)	95,787,121
Christianity		1	6917	1398	1146	9462	22,879 (2,603)	4640 (809)	1,756,583
Others	53	35	17,954	22,216	1013	41,271	99,499 (74)	157,114 (77)	10,242,730
Total	81,327	77,152	33,370	27,417	7337	226,597			214,028,032

(Japanese ministry of cultural affairs, March 2001)

Usually we consider religion to be a matter of unwavering personal conviction. But in Japan a single family, or even individual, can profess more than one religion, and mix and match them according to specific needs. For example, if you were to ask young Japanese which religion their family practised, many would say Buddhism. However, many would find it difficult to specify the specific sect – only at times such as the funeral of a grandparent would this information be realized. In recent years, many urban families have chosen to use commercial funeral homes where funerals are conducted on a commercial basis with only some consideration regarding religious preferences – many participants do not recognize which Buddhist denomination is used for the ceremony.

Rites of passage give a hint of the pluralism which exists in contemporary Japan. A hundred days after the birth of a child many families have a Shinto blessing ceremony. At age three, five and seven, families take their children, usually dressed in traditional costume, back to the shrine for celebrations and prayers. At the same time many of these families send their children to Christian kindergartens or nursery schools where they are happy to sing carols at Christmas and take part in seasonal festivities. Prior to taking university

entrance exams, many high school students and their parents
go to particular Shinto shrines, known for the emphasis they
place on academic teaching, to buy *umae* – wooden cards on
which to write a prayer asking for success in the examination. The Kitano Shrine in Kyoto is one such shrine, famous
for the divine favours it is reputed to bestow upon entrance
examination students. It contains a shrine to Michizane Sug-
awara, a "divine academic", who died in 903.

Through the course of their lives, people visit different
Shinto shrines and Buddhist temples for particular divine
favours. For example, for well-being in marriage one goes to
the Izumo Taisha (Matsue); for a safe birth, to the Nakayama
Temple (between Osaka and Kobe) for safety on the road, the
Narita Temple (outside Tokyo); and for prosperity in busi-

New Religions in Japan

Religion	Founded	1958	1990	2000
Old New Religion Tenrikyo	1838	2,047,708	1,839,009	1,758,436
Kurozumikyo	1814	751,770	295,225	319,702
Konkokyo	1859	619,625	442,584	430,190
Ennokyo	1919	108,200	419,452	461,243
Nichiren Group Soka Gakkai	1930	n/a	17,639,866	8,210,000*
Reiukai	1925	3,465,688	3,202,172	1,702,686
Rissho Kosei Kai	1938	1,349,905	6,348,120	5,742,564
Other Group Omoto	1892	93,535	172,460	172,094
Seicho no Ie	1930	1,533,784	838,496	850,435
Sekai Kyuseikyo	1934	395,240	835,756	835,756
P. L. Kodan	1924	701,550	1,289,064	1,117,408

(Japanese ministry of cultural affairs, 1991 and 2001)

*(number of households)

ness, the Ebisu Shrine (Osaka). Then, at a death, many families return to Buddhism for the funeral and traditional memorial services after one, three, seven, thirteen, twenty-three and fifty years.

There are, of course, variations and exceptions. But these examples indicate both the degree of religious tolerance and ambiguity that exist in Japan. While this can be seen in a positive light, there is also uncertainty regarding religious commitment at the personal level. The superficial picture of religious prosperity in Japan – a plethora of religious festivals and observances – has to be weighed against the ambiguity individuals must experience as they shift religious devotion.

As the table shows, over the last 150 years Japan has seen a rise in new religions. Some are the reformulation of traditional religions, others are entirely new. Three main phases of growth can be distinguished, coinciding with periods of social crisis and modernization. The first period occurred around the period of the Meiji Restoration (1868). This marked the great shift from a feudal society to a modern one. Religions, such as Tenrikyo and Konkokyo which derive from the Shinto tradition, date from this time.

The second phase immediately followed the second world war. In defeat, many Japanese experienced not only physical and economic destruction of cities and livelihoods but also crisis in their spiritual life and moral values. While some of the new religions, such as Soka Gakkai and Rissho Koseikai, which are based on Nichiren Buddhism, developed before the war they only really flourished after it. With charismatic leaders these new religious groups organized lay movements, mainly among migrants newly arrived in the big cities from rural areas. These people had left their traditional homelands and, their old religions and in the vacuum created, the new religions spread.

The last twenty years have seen the latest phase in the growth of the new religions. While Japan has made spectacular strides in its economic and technological development, serious social and personal crises have arisen, especially during downturns in the economy. One of the new religions, Omu (a radical new sect with a Buddhist background) is a notable example – followers of this religion were behind the gas attack on the Tokyo subway in 1995. Omu centres on the charismatic personality of Shoko Asahara and encourages a mind control system which has led some of its followers to engage in violent action. The big question, however, is how have some of the most highly educated graduates been attracted by this and other extreme sects? This question chal-

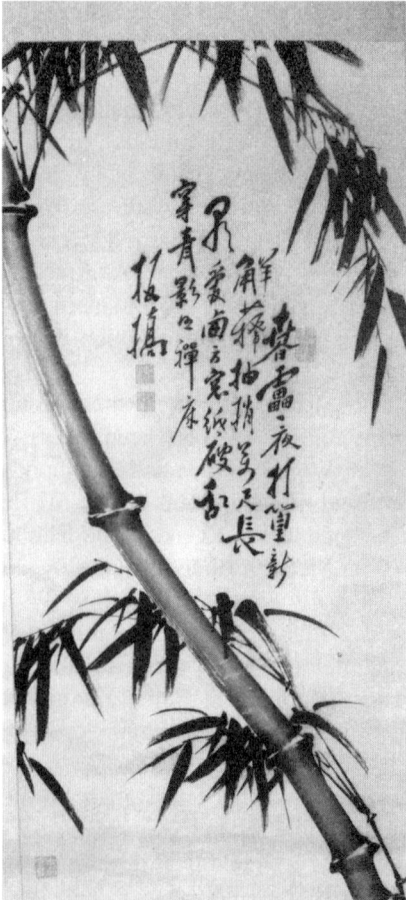

Bamboo *by Cheng Hang Kyo*

lenges the whole educational system, as well as families, schools and communities in Japan.

Returning to our subject, bamboo – it is considered to symbolize the spirit of loyalty. The image of a bamboo stem is used to represent loyalty – the straight stem of the bamboo acting as a symbol for loyalty. Before the second world war – an ultra-nationalist period – loyalty to the emperor was absolute. In the post-war period, the company took the place of the monarchy and people gave their all for which ever company they worked for. In today's society increasing emphasis is being placed on individual identity, and loyalty to one's self is newly stressed. Bamboo reminds us where to place our loyalty. On whom do you bestow your ultimate loyalty?

Here are two pictures of bamboo. One was painted by Cheng Hang Kyo (19th century), a distinguished Chinese calligrapher. When the Shin, who came from the north, overran Cheng's folk, the Han, they demanded that he draw a picture of orchid. He drew an orchid with dry roots – without any of the soil of his Han homeland. He also drew bamboo growing vigorously – expressing the spirit of bamboo; its characteristic strong steady growth despite the strong winds and storms that batter it.

The work of Sentaro Nanba (1865–1945) is less well known. He was a protestant minister serving a small congregation in the northern Japan. While engaging in his pastoral work, he produced poems, essays, brush paintings and calligraphy. He made a deep impression on the heart of both Christian and non-Christian friends in the areas where he served. He frequently wrote poems on bamboo and painted pictures on bamboo. He expressed his appreciation on bamboo with four characters, Clean Joint and Common Root. Through his story and those of other figures I have discerned five characteristics about the relationships between Christians and people of other faiths in Japan.

Local cultural expression

Mokugetsu combined traditional poetry with calligraphy and was able to vividly express his message. Sometimes the

Clean Joint and
Common Root
*by Mokugetsu
(Sentaro Nanba)*

message was explicitly Christian, as when he quoted scripture; at other times he took a non-religious theme, such as a
flower in the field, but treated it in the light of Christian faith.

On a visit to Romania at the invitation of Romanian
Orthodox Church, I was impressed by the beautiful architecture, which sat harmoniously in the landscape of gently
rolling hillsides. A common motif, found under the eaves,

was that of three ropes plaited together (often seen carved in wood). The rope, a common item with these former hunting and horse-riding people, was being used creatively to express trinitarian faith.

There are numerous other examples from Asia. For example when flower arrangements in Japan are used to express the Christian faith (Masao Takenaka and Megumi Yoshida, *Consider the Flowers: Meditations in Ikebana*, 1990), or, in Taiwan, where a fishing community has made creative use of local symbols such as fish and boats in designing their church (Masao Takenaka, *The Place Where God Dwells: An Introduction to Church Architecture in Asia*, 1995). As stated in Corinthians 4:7, "we have this treasure in earthen vessels", so we receive the gift of God in earthen vessels – local cultural artefacts.

Learning from one another

If radical monotheism means believing that God's grace works through all realms of creation and history, we have to raise the question of what God is doing among the people of other faiths. Mokugetsu made many friends, both Christians and others. This group of people not only enjoyed each others company but they also shared a mutual appreciation of the gifts of truth and beauty. Despite different backgrounds and culture people can share a common appreciation of experiences. At the age of 75, near the end of his life, Mokugetsu was invited to visit Shunsho Hirata, the chief abbot of Rengeji Temple (Takeno, northwest of Kyoto). He and his wife stayed for nearly two months, and painted more than a hundred pictures for the sliding screens in the temple. The themes he painted were common subjects, such as pine trees, mountains, birds, flowers and vegetables. The pictures – the work of a Christian pastor in a Buddhist temple – are placed on every screen and wall of the temple and are a popular attraction. Mokugetsu refused any fee for his work so the abbot had a memorial built in 1940 to honour him. It still stands today as a testament to friendship and mutual appreciation.

Screen painting by Mokugetsu at Rengeji Temple

Shared values can cross the boundaries of religion and time. An example comes from the life of Mahatma Gandhi. When studying law in London Gandhi read Tolstoy's *The Kingdom of God Is Within You* and was inspired by Tolstoy's message of non-violence. He then went on to read for the first time the *Bhagavad Gita*, a core text of his own faith – Hinduism. Later, when working in South Africa he established an *ashram* for the oppressed India population and called it Tolstoy Farm. Martin Luther King, in turn was inspired by Gandhi's writings on non-violent resistance.

Going back to Tolstoy (1828–1910), we discover that he was the son of a rich aristocrat concerned only with the material pleasures of life and worldly fame. At the age of 52, he had a spiritual conversion and turned his back on his family, wealth and position in society to adopt a life of non-violence, asceticism and service. He became an ardent follower of the teachings of the Sermon on the Mount. His *Confession*, written in his early fifties, describes his encounter with an Eastern folktale. A traveller was being chased by a wild beast and fell into a well. Clinging to a bush to survive he saw beneath him a ravenous dragon. The bush's roots were being nibbled away by two mice. The story deeply impressed Tolstoy as a portrait of transient nature of human life. This story is widely travelled and translated. It originates from an episode in the life of Buddha and has been transmitted to Europe via Muslim sources.

Throughout history religious people have shared common values and exchanged ideas and aspirations down the ages and across the continents.

It is a never-ending story. For example, Gandhi, as well as being inspired by Tolstoy, was impressed with Henry David Thoreau's essay on civil disobedience. In his turn, Gandhi's ideas had a great an impact on Dietrich Bonhoeffer. The Mahatma's way of life inspired Bonhoeffer's sermon on "Peace" at Fanø, Denmark in 1934. "Are we to be put to shame by heathens in the East? Are we to desert those individuals who have staked their lives on this message?" Bonhoeffer's influence can be widely seen in Japan. All of Bonhoeffer's major works and a four-volume biography have been translated into Japanese.

I can still vividly remember my feelings when I read the *Cost of Discipleship* for the first time. I was then, in 1949, a student at the school of theology, Doshisha University.

Reflecting on Bonhoeffer's impact in Japan, I recollect one occasion when I was taking a Western theologian to Tenruji Temple, the chief temple of one of the Zen sects, in Kyoto, to visit the chief abbot, Seiko Hirata. After we had enjoyed a cup of green tea, the conversation turned to the history of the temple and the meaning of Zen practice. The abbot asked, "May I raise a question?" We said, "Yes, please." To our surprise, he said, partly in German, "What does it mean when Dietrich Bonhoeffer says, *Vor und mit Gott leben wir ohne Gott?*" (Before and with God we live without God). I ventured to offer my own interpretation in terms of an eclipse of the sun, during which we act as if the sun does not exist even though we know the sun exists. He nodded and asked further, "It is interesting. I would like to know whether this kind of interpretation is a minority opinion or a majority opinion among Christian theologians?" I said, "I guess we are a minority but we are a growing minority."

So the sense of shared appreciation continues to echo through the ages – from the story of the Buddha through Muslim teachings to Tolstoy to Gandhi to Bonhoeffer, and the interest of a Zen priest in Japan. This common understanding does not mean that we abandon our respective points of view. We can look at this universal application of grace in the light of radical monotheism. More specifically, in accepting the crucified and risen Christ we can come to the wider view that divine grace operates in all realms of life, including in peoples of other faiths and of no faith.

Let me here recite a poem, which Bonhoeffer composed during the dark days when he was held as a prisoner of war in Germany living with people of many different backgrounds and faiths.

Christians and unbelievers

> Men go to God when they are sore bestead,
> Pray to him for succour, for his peace, for bread,
> For mercy for them sick, sinning or dead:
> All men do so, Christian and unbelieving.
>
> Men go to God when he is sore bestead,
> Find him poor and scorned, without shelter or bread,
> Whelmed under weight of the wicked, the weak, the dead:
> Christians stand by God in his hour of grieving.
>
> God goeth to every man when sore bestead,
> Feedeth body and spirit with his bread,
> For Christians, heathens alike he hangeth dead:
> And both alike forgiving.

(Dietrich Bonhoeffer, *Widerstand und Ergebung*, 1955, English version, *Letters and Papers from Prison*, transl. Eberhard H. Fuller, London, SCM Press, 1953).

The World Council of Churches launched its programme for the Decade to Overcome Violence in February 2001, to bring justice and reconciliation through non-violent action. This cause is a very important aspect of the ecumenical calling today. As Bonhoeffer said the work of God through Christ is directed to both Christian and non-Christian alike. The fact that we are all recipients of God's love and forgiveness is the basis for joint action for peace and justice in the world.

Critical assessment

When reviewing the history of religious institutions we find continuous conflicts and divisions, either on doctrinal or political matters. However, when studying the history of religious people we find ample examples of cross-fertilization of beliefs and ideas. While religious institutions may foster division, religious people promote interaction and learning.

In the preaching of Paul in the Areopagus, a meeting place in Athens where people of different backgrounds exchanged ideas (Acts 17:16–28), the various groups, "Jews and devout persons", "the Epicurean and Stoic philosophers" met with Paul. The passage continues, "Now all the Athenians and the foreigners who lived there spent their time in nothing except telling or hearing something new." They asked Paul to tell them of his beliefs. After recognizing the religious diversity in Athens he raised a critical question about the idols he had seen. "I found also an alter with this inscription, 'To an unknown god.' What therefore you worship is unknown." Then he proclaimed, "The God who has made the world and everything in it, being Lord of heaven and earth, does not live in shrines made by man, nor is he served by human hands." Based on the faith in the transcendent God revealed in Jesus Christ, Paul presents the universal presence of God by saying, "He made from one every nation of men to live on all of the face of the earth, having determined allotted periods and the boundaries of their habitation." And he goes on to say, "Yet he is not far from each one of us, for 'In him we live and move and have our being.'" This passage is important in indicating the basis of radical monotheism; we enter into joint work with the people of other faiths in every sphere of the world.

Acting together

A fourth characteristic of the relationship between Christians and people of other faiths or no faith is that of joint action. As citizens of the global community we share common problems. It is important that religious people not only encourage each other, lifting up their consciousness, but also work together for peace, justice and the integrity of creation.

A case study illustrating the power of cooperation is that of Dharavi, in Bombay, India. Dharavi is an area of approximately two square kilometres sandwiched between the railway line and the Mitha River; about 300,000 people live there. Through the efforts of the Urban and Rural Mission of the Christian Conference of Asia, a democratic community organization called PROUD (People's Responsible Organization of United Dharavi) was established in 1980. It aimed to encourage people's democratic participation in working for basic rights for land, housing, water, sanitation, employment and other needs that directly relate to the welfare, safety and well-being of the people of Dharavi. One of the significant factors in the process of community organization was all religions – Hindus, Muslims, Buddhists, Christians and others – participated. While religious organizations and institutions quite often find themselves in competition and even conflict, religious people can work effectively together for common goals.

Another, more recent, example comes from the Kyoto climate change conference held in 1998. The Association of Centres for Social Concern in Asia organized an inter-religious consultation on environmental issues. People from different religious communities – Hindu, Muslim, Buddhist and Christian – expressed their views on environmental issues. Towards the end of the consultation, the religious participants of the conference joined together, at the main cathedral to offer prayers. After listening to the message of Raul Estrada-Oyuela, a conference moderator and Catholic layperson from Argentina, everyone marched down the main street of Kyoto while the temple bells of the city rang to express common prayer and commitment. This event was special in two ways. First, there was the inter-religious cooperation and, secondly, it was planned and carried jointly by various religious organizations: the Kyoto Religious Federation, the Japan Committee of the World Conference on Religion and Peace, the Central Council of Catholic Church in Japan and the National Christian Council of Japan.

Self-renewal

The final aspect, characterizing the links between Christians and people of other faiths or no faith is the concern for the renewal of oneself. Opportunities to encounter others allow you to assess yourself and your own situation in a new light – present an opportunity for self-renewal.

As previously mentioned, Tolstoy turned his life around through reading a story that came from the East. This didn't make him a Buddhist but the encounter allowed him to take the biblical message seriously. Similarly, after Gandhi was inspired by Tolstoy's writing, he rediscovered the non-violent way of life *(ahimsa)* extolled in ancient Hindu texts to which he had not previously paid attention.

A related story from my own life involves a priest, named Fusetsu Ogata, from one of Kyoto's Buddhist temples belonging to the Nichiren (Buddhist) sect. After an interfaith conference in Tokyo, as we were returning home together on the Shinkansen (Bullet Train) back to Kyoto, we became friends. He began to attend the meetings we held at Kansai Seminar House and in turn, I was invited to visit his temple. One time at the temple, I asked, "Where is the image of the Buddha?" To my great surprise he answered, "There is no image of Buddha here." I asked, "Why not?" He said, "I learned this from the Judeo-Christian religion, which rejects idol worship." He took me to the sanctuary where he had placed the text of the Lotus Sutra (the teachings of Buddha) at the worship centre. This radical change, replacing the image of Buddha with the Lotus Sutra, had resulted in the loss of several of the temple's influential parishioners. In order to overcome the financial crisis this caused, his wife had started a nursery. "That's why I have to be obedient to my wife's command," he laughed. When I asked about his daily routine, he told me that he usually got up at 3.30 in the morning to copy the four texts of the major religions: the Old Testament, the New Testament, the Koran and the Lotus Sutra. He had started this practice in order to promote joint work between world religions through mutual understanding and intercessory prayer. I asked furthermore, "Why have you included the Koran, the text of Islam?" He replied, "When I read Kanzo Uchimura's *Japan and the Japanese* (1894) (describing five key religious Japanese figures), I was impressed. Uchimura included Nichiren (a 13th-century reformer) in his five representative men of Japan. He regarded him highly, not only as the founder of the Nichiren sect, but also as a prophetic figure who fought the corruption and hypocrisy of his time." The priest had come to be interested in Mohammed because Uchimura had said Nichiren was as if Mohammed himself had come to Japan. Around the time that Uchimura wrote his book he surveyed biographies of outstanding people. He had been especially interested in Thomas Carlyle's work, *On Heroes, Hero-worship and the Heroic in History*. Carlyle included the life of Mohammed and portrayed his beliefs.

And so, every morning after reading texts from four different religions, this Buddhist priest would write down his reflections about those texts and distribute them to his friends in various religious communities. Crossing time and space, this process of cross-fertilization and self-reflection and renewal is going on in many parts of the world. It is interesting to realize that it also brings about transformation and conversion, under the guidance of the Holy Spirit.

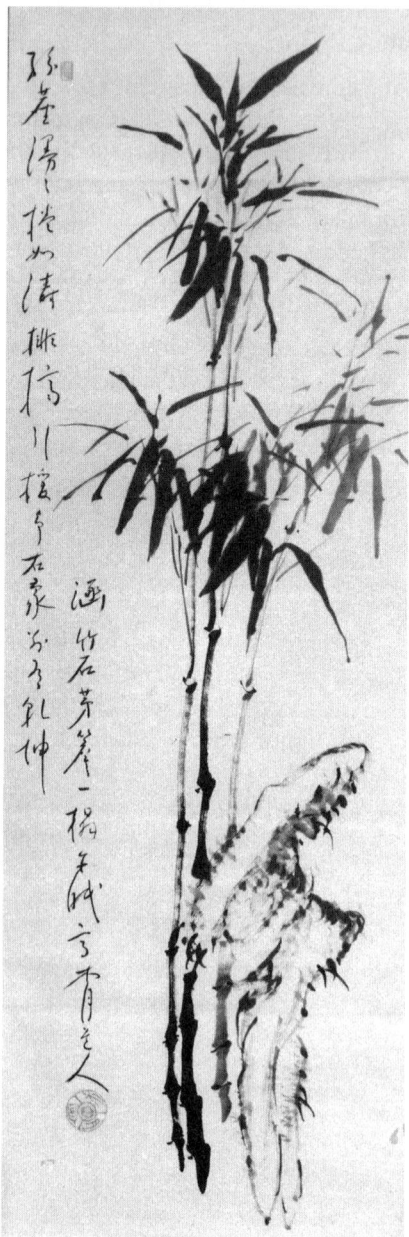

Bamboo beside the Rock, *Mokugetsu (Sentaro Nanba), painting in* sumi

4. Clean Wind and Bending Stem

We now come to the heart of the book, where we consider the spirituality of bamboo. It is a Japanese cultural tradition to think of nature as a "companion" rather than something to conquer. There are three plants – pine, bamboo and plum – used as "friends" in this respect. Of the three, bamboo is especially cherished for the deep spirituality with which it is imbued. In many Zen temples bamboo is found both in the garden and utilized in *shoin* (studies) where pictures are employed. In his book *Zen and Japanese Culture*, Daisets T. Suzuki points out that bamboo is mentioned in many common Zen sayings, such as "willows are green and flowers red", "bamboo is straight and the pine is gnarled". According to Suzuki, while drawing a bamboo one forgets oneself and becomes a bamboo. He calls this process a "rhythmic movement of the spirit", which resides in the bamboo as well as in the artist.

Ryokan (1758–1831), one of the most popular Zen priests, trained at the Entsuji Temple in the Okayama, southern Honshu. He then chose to become a mendicant priest in the snow-covered Niigata region in the north, instead of becoming a senior priest at a temple. Through poetry and calligraphy he expressed his affinity for the simple life full of the companionship of ordinary Japanese. He is as respected as St Francis of Assisi (1181–1226). Commemorating the 170th anniversary of Ryokan's death in May 2000, a new Noh drama, *Wings of Love*, composed by Yuko Yuasa, was performed in the cultural centre of Niigata. Ryokan lived in a simple hermitage called Gogo-an on Mount Kugami. He enjoyed the bamboo grove which surrounded his hut. He appreciated the spiritual qualities of bamboo, with its roots firmly set in the ground and leaves green the year round, calling forth a fresh wind. He also enjoyed tasting its fresh young shoots in the spring. There is a story which confirms his appreciation of bamboo. One day he saw a new young shoot sprouting through the floor of his room. He continued to watch it grow until one day, once it reached the ceiling, he started to remove the roof. In so doing, accidentally, the roof caught fire and the entire house, including the bamboo, burned down. Obsessed by something we hold dear, we can find ourselves doing something stupid.

Now we will move on to reflect on the spiritual meaning of bamboo in the light of the Christian faith. We have learned how bamboo is widely used in Japan; how it is an intimate companion in daily life – part of the environment as well as a practical tool. But it also promotes spirituality in Japan's cultural life. As a Japanese Christian I can identify four main strands of this important aspect of bamboo.

Bamboo, *calligraphy by Abbot Sadayasu, Daitokuji Temple, Kyoto*

Bamboo groves invite a clean wind

In many temples and shrines in Japan there is a bamboo grove. It is grown partly for the protection it affords the temple yard; it provides a natural defence against storms and earthquakes. But it also invites a clean wind.

The calligraphy reads:

For you bamboo brings clean wind with its green leaves.

There is a similar Japanese expression:

Clean winds gradually come and go through bamboo groves.

Another calligraphic work which illustrates the connection of bamboo with a clean wind is the work of Mokugetsu, a Christian minister mentioned in chapter 3. The poem reads:

On sunny days and rainy days
In winter and in summer
Every day good
Clean wind ever fresh
Green leaves overflow spirit

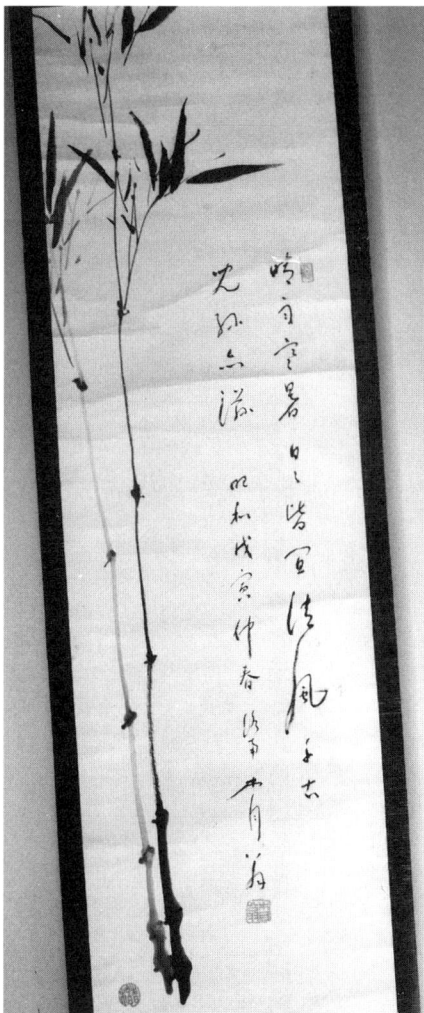

Bamboo, Clean Wind,
Ever Fresh,
*Mokugetsu (Sentaro
Nanba), painting in*
sumi

Mokugetsu also painted two friends talking together in a bamboo grove. As mentioned in chapter 1, in China there is a story of seven wise men who meet in a bamboo grove to enjoy both the clean wind the bamboo catches and a good discussion. The story is known as *Chikurin no shichi Kenjin* (Seven Wise Men in the Bamboo Grove).

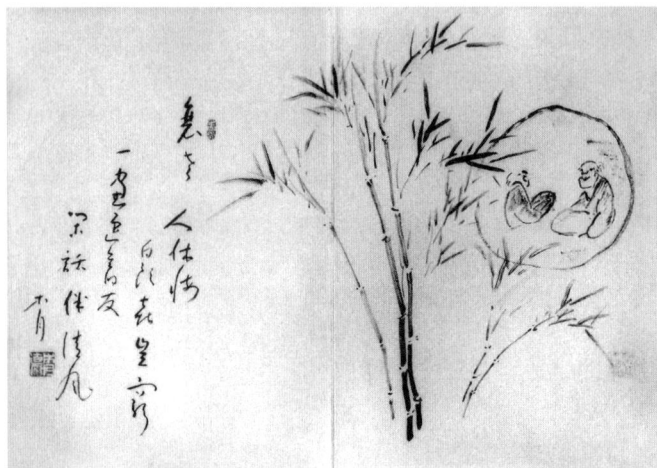

Two Friends in a Bamboo Grove, *Mokugetsu (Sentaro Nanba), painting in* sumi

In the biblical tradition the wind symbolizes the work of the Holy Spirit. When Nicodemus, a Pharisee, secretly came to Jesus by night, he asked, "How can a man be born when he is old?" Jesus replied, "Unless one is born of water and the Spirit, he cannot enter the kingdom of God." Nicodemus is referring to physical birth and wants to know, "Can he enter a second time into his mother's womb and be born again?" Jesus, however, replies at a spiritual level. He points out, "The wind blows where it will, and you hear the sound of it, but you do not know whence it comes or whither it goes; so it is with every one who is born of the Spirit" (John 3:1–8). This passage resonates with the Japanese mind because it closely resembles Zen dialogue; speaking of the spirit in terms of wind. We cannot see the wind and we do not know from where it comes or where it goes; the same is true of the spirit. A bamboo grove invites a clean wind – it reminds us of the work of the Holy Spirit.

The wind invited by bamboo is a clean one – it is a soft, tender, clean wind. We have observed how the art of the tea ceremony is intimately connected with bamboo. The tea house is usually surrounded by a bamboo grove. To enter the tea house one must go through a bamboo gate. Inside, the tea house is decorated with and supported by bamboo poles. Many of the utensils used in the tea ceremony are made of bamboo, such as the teaspoon, *(chashaku)*, tea whisk *(chasen)*, and ladle *(hishaku)*.

Chasen *(tea whisk)*

The tea ceremony also uses other bamboo items, such as the *kekkai* (a bamboo pole used to mark out the floor), which is used to demarcate guest from host, the *futaoki* (rest for the kettle lid), and the *hanair* (flower basket). It seems that without bamboo there would be no tea ceremony!

There are several reasons why bamboo is used so widely. Partly, it is readily available and inexpensive. Equally important is its simple beauty. However, its main property is its purity and spirituality. Bamboo not only invites a clean wind but it also encourages a pure spirit when used for practical everyday applications.

There are four basic principles in the tradition of *Cha-do* (the way of tea) which are summarized in the teachings of Senno Rikyu (1522–1591), the founder of *Cha-do*. The four principles are (1) *wa* – harmony, (2) *kei* – respect and appreciation, (3) *sei* – cleanness and purity, and (4) *jaku* – solitude and tranquillity.

Soshitsu Sen, Grand Tea Master XV, helped to rebuild the tea house at Kansai Seminar House, Kyoto in 1982. He called the house Seishin-an (Pure Heart Tea House). He consciously related one of the principles of the "way of tea" to

Pure Heart Tea House, Kansai Seminar House, Kyoto

the biblical text, "Blessed are the pure in heart, for they shall see God" (Matt. 5:8).

"Cleanliness and orderliness, in both the physical and spiritual sense, are a very important part of the study of Tea, as in Zen training in general. In Zen, even the most mundane acts – washing dishes or cleaning floors – are the seeds of enlightenment. When the host cleans his utensils he is simultaneously purifying his heart and mind through his total concentration on his task. Before entering the tea hut, guests pass along a garden path and then rinse their hands and wash out their mouths at a low stone water-basin, thereby symbolically purifying themselves of the 'dust' of the everyday world outside in tea-room. *Sei* (part of its name) means purity. The way in which the stone steps in the garden path are arranged is another example of the simplicity found there" (*The Philosophy of Cha-do, The Urasenke Tradition of Tea*).

The cleanliness striven for in the tea ceremony is both spiritual and physical – a pure mind and a clean, simple space. It is interesting to note that the grand tea master, Soshitsu Sen, named the tea-room of the Kansai Seminar House "Pure Heart Tea House", due in part to this traditional principle of cleanliness but also no doubt related to his student days at Doshisha University where he studied the beatitudes in the Sermon on the Mount.

Throughout the history of Christian thought "Blessed are the pure in heart, for they shall see God" (Matt. 5:8) has inspired many people. In fact, K.E. Kirk (a distinguished moral philosopher from Britain) goes so far as to describe the history of Christian ethics as the history of people who have been inspired by this very line (*The Vision of God: The Christian Doctrine of the "Summum Bonum"*). In his research on visions of God through history, Kirk includes not only Jewish sources but also such non-Christian philosophers Plato and the mystics Eleusis and Philo of Alexandria.

Kirk points to two types of approach evident through history. Take for example the development of monasteries. The "formalist" approach which, it can be argued, started with the codification of the New Testament and manifested itself in the development of monastic orders, suggests that in order to see God one must follow the Commandments – a set of rules. Another approach is the "rigorous" one, whereby extreme effort is extorted as the way to see God. By this approach, ascetics taking to the wilderness are seen as the founding fathers of monasteries. In the middle ages, as the formalization of monasticism continued, there was also a rise of rigorous mission-oriented movements, such as St Francis of Assisi in the 12th century. Kirk views the history of Christian ethics as a dialectical seesaw between these two approaches.

The duality and tension between these two approaches – formalism and rigorism – can also be seen in the religious history of Japan. At the height of the growth of Buddhism in the middle ages monasteries were developed. After came "rigorous" attempts to enact reforms and to engage in missionary service and witness among people in need. There have always been tensions between these two approaches. During the time Buddhism became formally established in the Kamakura period (1185–1333), Nichiren (1222–82) made reforms through rigorous prophetic and missionary work among the people. Although he was exiled to Sado Island, he had a deep influence. He trained disciples who later went on to establish the Nichiren sect, which to this day plays a significant role in Japanese society. From the Nichiren sect new religions, such as Sokagakkai and Risshokoseikai, have arisen. With his background in the traditional Tendai sect, Dogen (1200–53) studied in China and with his rigorous approach founded the Eiheiji Temple, which became the main temple of Soto Zen. Ryokan (1751–1831), who belonged to the Soto Zen sect trained for 18 years at Entsuji and then became a mendicant priest engaging in a simple life and expressing himself through poetry and calligraphy.

In the Christian community in Japan there have been several mystics who rigorously sought a vision of God. One of these was Tadayoshi Hara (1865–1907), one of the earliest graduates of Doshisha. After undertaking dedicated mission work in the snow-covered Niigata region, he spent the year before his death trying to rehabilitate his health. While doing so, he published a book entitled *The Union of God and Man*, in which he tells of his personal experience of the mystical union with God. Ryosen Tsunashima (1873–1907), who taught ethics at Waseda University, in Tokyo, is another example. In the latter part of his life, while sick in bed, he wrote several essays describing his visions of God. Yet another mystic, Seitaro Yoshida (1863–1950), throughout his life disciplined himself to pursue a life of purity seeking a vision of God. It is interesting to note that although Yoshida remained a committed Christian pastor in a small church in Tokyo throughout his life, he maintained good relationships with people of other faiths, especially Zen Buddhism.

We started our spiritual search by reflecting on the phrase "the bamboo grove invites a clean wind". We have come to recognize the indispensable importance of having inner discipline in our everyday lives. As Bonhoeffer expresses, so well, in his teachings: "Arcane discipline without worldliness is a ghetto and worldliness without arcane discipline is no more than the streets."

Here, I would like to recall the significant influence Osui Arai (1846–1922) had on the life of Shozo Tanaka (1841–1913). Tanaka was a well-known peasant leader who campaigned tirelessly against the pollution emitted from the Ashio Copper mine in Tochigi, north of Tokyo. In the early days of industrialization this was not an easy cause to fight, since both national government and local authorities considered economic development their top priority and very few people cared about the effects of pollution. Tanaka likened his own life of struggle to that of a rain and wind beaten ox, leaving nothing but wheel tracks in the mud. Yet somehow he found the spiritual resources to continue his work. He wrote in his diary on 24 December 1912:

> To care for the mountain, your heart must be a mountain.
> To care for the river, your heart must be a river.

Tanaka was elected by the village people to political office in the district assembly and later as a member of the national parliament. Unable to achieve his goal of stopping the pollution, he resigned from political office and went to the village of Yanaka, one of the polluted areas, to live with the people affected. It is said that when he died, at the age of 72, in his pocket he was carrying both the Japanese constitution and the gospel according to Matthew. Five years after his death, the district court ruled in support of the appeal of the Yanaka villagers.

Who taught the Bible to Shozo Tanaka? He started reading the Bible when he was in prison in 1902. A recent study has shown that Osui Arai was the one who acted as a father figure and provided spiritual succour. Whenever Tanaka was worn out he would come to visit Osui Arai at Kenwasha (House of Humility and Harmony) in the northern part of Tokyo. He would welcome Tanaka with a hot bath, good food and rest, after which they would share the message of the Bible. These were periods of physical and spiritual refreshment and renewal.

Osui Arai was from the Sendai clan – who were defeated at the time of the Meiji Restoration in 1868. He and his friends left the clan which had decided to surrender to the Emperor. They fled to Hakaidate, Hokkaido, in the north, where Osui Arai came under the influence of Kasatkin Nikolij (1836–1912), a missionary from the Russian Orthodox Church. Later he went to the United States and lived in a community under the guidance of Thomas Lake Harris (1823–1906) who was a mystical universalist. Arai never married and refused to have his photograph taken during his life; he also commanded his disciples to make no cemetery or tomb for him after his death. He left a powerful prayer in which he addressed God not as Our Father but as Mother-Father God.

> Inward prayer
> O God, the One-in-Twain, the Two-in-One! Strengthen us by Thy kindling breath, that we may rise unto Thee in the Divine fire and flame.
>
> O Lord! We have this day but one consciousness – the consciousness of serving Thee.
>
> We beseech Thee, our Mother-Father, whatever is of *necessity* – that which must be done – for the service of Thy New Life, let us be conscious of it and be doing it, this day, tomorrow, always!
>
> Most gracious and merciful Lord-Lady, our Saviour-Saviouress! Let us forget all that which for the ends of Thy service we should forget. But we pray Thee to wake us up, faculty by faculty, ever in Thee; so that we may remember, in unison and harmony, whatever is requisite for the service of Thy Saviourhood.

The flexibility of bamboo

One of the distinctive characteristics of bamboo is its flexibility. The bamboo grove bends before a strong wind but never collapses. It exhibits an amazing pliability without surrendering its sustaining spirit. The bamboo grove certainly invites a clean wind. It is usually a soft and tender wind. But sometimes it meets a strong wind or even a snowstorm. It bends before the wind yet comes back again and again, demonstrating its stamina and flexibility. The picture of

Bamboo beside the rocks, by an unknown artist, shows the plant's ability to withstand strong winds. The scene is set at the seashore where prevailing winds are strong. The bamboo bends under the wind but springs back again and again. This characteristic has been applied practically, for example, in using bamboo for bows in archery.

Bamboo beside the Rocks, unknown artist

This leads on to the consideration of two significant ethical virtues, namely loyalty and hope. The fact that bamboo stands up straight brings the virtue of loyalty to mind. In chapter 3, the picture in *sumi* by Mokugetsu, *Clean Joint and Common Root,* is a classic example of the oriental tradition of combining painting and poetry, image and message, for full expression. To understand such material both the right side and the left side of the brain need to work together simultaneously. This is also recognized in the Bible: as Jesus said, "Blessed are your eyes, for they see, and your ears, for they hear" (Matt. 13:16). This phenomenon is widespread in today's world – television, internet, books, theatre, advertising.

Elaborating further: to understand the meaning of "clean joint", for "joint" one must read "loyalty". An image of bamboo standing straight conveys loyalty. The virtue of loyalty has been emphasized by Confucian ethics, especially in relation to loyalty to the lord whom one serves. This sense of loyalty, in serving one's master, was strongly encouraged during the feudal period and re-enforced during the nationalist era (1894–1945) where the people served the emperor. Since the second world war it is loyalty to a company that has taken the place of rulers. In Japan collective loyalty to a person or institution has been the predominant trend rather than the individualism of the West, where emphasis is placed on the importance of one's own values.

Josiah Royce (1855–1916) developed the theme of loyalty in his book, *The Philosophy of Loyalty*. In the course of his discussions, he examines the idea of loyalty through the notion of "loyalty to loyalty" He analyzes the grounds on which questions of loyalty are decided. Where do you place ultimate loyalty? Religion provides the best foundations for loyalty.

In Christian faith we are dealing with God not only in terms of loyalty to God but also in terms of God's loyalty to humanity. "God so loved the world that he gave his only son that whoever believes in him should not perish but have eternal life" (John 3:16). And so, our loyalty to God is in response to God's loyalty to us. The clean wind through the bamboo grove reminds us of the loyalty of God which is the basis for our own loyalty to God.

Another important spiritual meaning of bamboo's flexibility is that it exemplifies hope. Bamboo may bend but it always rises again, it never gives up. The question of hope is one of the most urgent religious questions in Japan today. In the post-war period, individualism has come to be pursued as a reaction against the ultra-nationalism which held sway before. Yet it does not take long to see the uncertainty of individuals in the midst of such a changing society. Especially after the economic bubble burst in the 1990s, anxiety and frustration prevailed. The economic depression that has shaken Japanese society over the last ten years has laid bare its deep worries and ambiguities, both at the individual and collective, societal level. This means that the question of hope has become a central issue.

This is the time to examine the capacity for hope that each individual possesses and to recognize its finite and temporary nature. As is said, "Now hope that is seen is not hope. For who hopes for what he sees? But if we hope for what we do not see, we wait for it with patience" (Rom. 8:24–25). The question of hope has been raised in the ecumenical movement several times. In Evanston in 1954 the theme was "Christ – the Hope of the World". In the Christian-Marxist dialogue between Ernst Bloch and Jürgen Moltmann, hope appeared to emerge as the result of nihilistic despair rather than from a more idealistic pursuit.

Here it is appropriate to consider the central theme of Shusaku Endo's work. He became a Christian through his mother, who was a Christian trying to bring her son into Christian faith. He saw that his faith came from his mother, rather like a ready-made Western garment. His mission is to convert this Western garment into a Japanese k*imono*. In his writings he takes up the question of loyalty. One may determine to be loyal to Christ, but be too weak to fulfil the call. In his work, *The Life of Jesus* (1973), he deals with the image of Jesus in a Japanese context. He portrays Jesus not as the powerful heroic Christ but as a powerless person among a weak people. It is an image of the suffering servant who is like a sheep, dumb before its shearers (Isa. 53:7).

The disciples, who expected Christ to be powerful, felt disappointed and betrayed. Peter, for example, made the courageous confession, "You are the Christ, the Son of the living God" (Matt. 16:16), but he was a weak man who was not able to maintain his loyalty to Jesus. Although he pledged his loyalty by saying, "Lord, I am ready to go with you to prison and to death" (Luke 22:33), he soon thereafter betrayed Jesus by denying him three times. The eyes of Jesus met Peter's as he "turned and looked at Peter" (Luke 22:61). To me, Jesus' turning to regard the weak, traitorous Peter is very impressive. We usually look straight to the front where the chief object of our attention is. Jesus must have had a special consideration for Peter to turn round to look at him. He did not regard Peter with accusing and critical eyes but with tender and merciful ones; it is as if he embraced him.

In the Eikando Temple, which stands at the foot of the Eastern Mountain in Kyoto, we can see the unique image of the Maitreya *bodhisattva*. It is called the Mikaeri-Miroku, the turning Maitreya. Here the Maitreya turns around to look at the person who is behind. Miroku is considered a *bodhisattva* (an enlightened being who has stayed on earth to help others attain salvation). It is interesting that despite the differences, both Buddhism and Christianity use the concept of turning around "to extend special mercy to those who are weak and betraying".

Maitreya bodhisattva
at Eikando Temple,
Kyoto

Endo depicts the theme of the misery caused by disloyalty in an early novel, *Silence* (1966). The novel is set at a time when Christians in Japan were severely persecuted and went underground. Their faith was tested by the authorities – they were asked to perform *fumie* (stepping on a sacred image of Christ). People would be called on and asked to step on the image. If they refused or even trembled, they were put in jail. In *Silence*, Endo describes the anxiety and pain caused by such persecution. Finally a priest is captured and tested. At first he resists. He is told that if he steps on it then three peasants being hung upside down in a hole will be released. He can hear the peasants groaning. Finally, he decides to tread on the image. He raises his foot over it and looks closely at the shape, distorted by having been stepped on by numbers of people. Then Christ, who had kept silent in spite of the ardent prayers of believers, speaks at last, "Trample! I know well the pain of your foot. Trample! I was born to be trampled by the people and it was in order to share the people's pain that I carried my cross."

Bronze fumie *tablet*

This story suggests that hope is possible, even at the very worst times. We are not talking about an idealistic hope, a hope for a transcendent future through either death or the dramatic end to history, but a hope based on God's presence in the midst of affliction. This hope comes from the belief that those who are weak and afflicted, even traitors, will be accepted and forgiven. They are embraced by transcendent grace and invited once again to live with one another in freedom and love.

Transcendental Dawn – Darkness and Wisdom, *1999, Yoko Magoshi*

Finally, on this theme I would like to refer a painting of Yoko Magoshi, a Japanese woman artist. In the painting she depicts great suffering. Dawn is coming but the sufferer sunk in darkness does not realize it. However, his friend is there to point out the coming of the dawn. This portrays existential hope based on transcendental light coming into the world. This image is closely related to the biblical message, "The light shines in the darkness, and the darkness has not overcome it. The true light that enlightens every man, was coming into the world. He was in the world, and the world was made through him, yet the world knew him not" (John 1:5,9,10). It also illustrates that one cannot find the light alone; that one needs a friend to help point the way.

The bending of the bamboo ably symbolizes the spirit of hope: it does not collapse but with great flexibility and perseverance it springs back and is renewed.

Green bamboo stem

5. Strong Roots and Empty Centre

Strong roots

We have considered the vitality of bamboo, which is often used as a symbol for life sustained in spite of suffering and oppression. Interestingly, on this theme, a book describing the history of the struggles of Japanese-Americans, Frank F. Chuman's *The Bamboo People: The Law and Japanese-Americans*, makes use of the symbol of bamboo. Chuman is a lawyer who has investigated the origins and development of the Japanese-American community and its relation to American legislation. The author himself is the son of a Japanese immigrant. Born in the United States in 1917, Chuman experienced the prejudice which was strong against the Japanese minority, evident in education, land ownership, legislation, and in internment during the second world war. Throughout his study he uses bamboo as an image to indicate the characteristics of Japanese-Americans.

"It is the bamboo which symbolizes the spirit of the Japanese people. We all know the fact that in spite of wind and storm the bamboo exhibits amazing flexible elasticity. In winter it bears heavy snow. Though it bends it does not fall down. It swings at the time of the storm yet when it is over, the bamboo return back to a straight position. It also symbolizes the practical character to be used in daily life in various ways."

One of the unique characteristics of bamboo can be found in its root system and strength. We ordinarily do not see the roots. Hidden from view, they are the source of the plant's vitality, as they stretch and grow, putting up new shoots. Prof. Hata Okamura's magnum opus, *Illustrated Horticultural Bamboo Species in Japan*, describes how bamboo grows.

It is well known that bamboo has strong roots which grow horizontally with amazing speed and strength. In Japanese there is an expression, *hachiku no ikioi*, which refers to the "irresistible force" of bamboo, even to the extent that it can break through walls. The saying also refers to bamboo roots stretching steadily, gradually increasing the size and strength of the plant.

Bamboo seldom flowers. Often a bamboo will flower only after 100 to 120 years. So, rather than through producing seeds, bamboo spreads via its roots. The roots develop differently depending on the type of bamboo. Some spread through their rootstock; some through subterranean stems (rhizomes); some combine both methods. In both cases, the root is the key determinant of growth. Dr Okamura depicts the stamina of bamboo through the power of its roots.

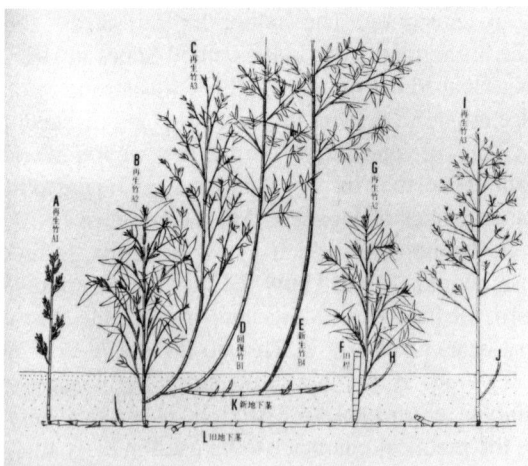

Diagram of bamboo root, Illustrated Horticultural Bamboo Species in Japan *by Hata Okamura*

H. Richard Niebuhr noted that many key theological terms contain the prefix "re-", as in regeneration, redemption, return, reconciliation, renewal and recreation. We are all created by God. Everything was good at the time of creation (Gen. 1:31). Then, after the fall we are all called to return to God to seek reconciliation in Christ (2 Cor. 5:19).

Saikontan is a story of root vegetables. It is a Chinese classic, published three hundred years ago. It tells of the importance of root vegetables such as the radish. It says, "If you eat my root everything will be accomplished. Superfluous flesh will spoil people's mind and body. The countryside will produce a clean people."

Painting in sumi *of a root vegetable by Mokugetsu*

The root of the bamboo is important both because of its physical effects and of its spiritual significance. To be stable, a human being needs solid roots. Today, in our rapidly changing world, rootlessness has become a critical ethical issue and social problem. Secularization and globalization make traditional values seem less and less relevant, and seem to encourage the rootlessness and lack of meaning that many people suffer in trying to live a life meeting the challenges of the present day. And, I would suggest, that individuals are more likely to find themselves holding ambiguous and ambivalent ethical beliefs as a result of this rootlessness. To be sure, we need to be flexible and open to challenges, but we also need to put down basic roots.

Simone Weil, writing during the second world war, was looking for a paradigm of the post-war period. She published her essays under the title of *The Need for Roots* in 1943. During the war she worked for the French government in exile in London and died from tuberculosis and malnutrition in a sanatorium in August 1943 at the age of 34. Although the essays are unfinished they contain constructive insights for the foundation of human life in post-war Europe. Its sub-title, *Prelude to a Declaration of Duties towards Mankind*, indicates that its central message is one of promoting human duty based on love and justice. Time has passed and conditions changed since these essays were written, but her point remains, that it is important to have roots in a time of reconstruction. I believe it is important to recognize Christ as the root of humanity:

> From now on, therefore, we regard no one from a human point of view; even though we once regarded Christ from a human point of view, we regard him thus no longer. Therefore, if anyone is in Christ, he is a new creation: the old has passed away, behold, the new has come. (2 Cor. 5:16–17)

Here, then, is our root as human beings. We are rooted not because of our own human efforts and strengths, but because Christ became human to achieve a ministry of reconciliation. Following him we humbly join in this ministry, so needed in our divided world.

Empty centre

Now we come to the most important aspect of the spirituality of bamboo, namely, the spirituality of emptiness. A bamboo stem is hollow. Biologically this factor is unusual; spiritually it contains deep meaning. In the Buddhist tradition, especially in Zen Buddhism, bamboo is highly regarded not only for bringing a fresh breeze, but also for promoting spiritual meditation. In Zen meditation the "bamboo centre shows emptiness". Achieving a state of mind of nothingness is one of the objectives of Zen meditation. Reaching a state of self-emptiness, especially in these increasingly self-centred and self-assertive days, is a hard goal to achieve. In our highly competitive societies one also wonders how one can live wisely by negating oneself. One sometimes needs to have the courage to be oneself.

Here it is important to acknowledge that the starting point of self-emptiness and humility is to understand our proper place before God, though not necessarily before others. In *Christ and Culture*, H. Richard Niebuhr wrote:

> The humility of Jesus is humility before God, and can only be understood as the humility of the son. He neither exhibited nor

commended or communicated the humility of inferiority-feeling before other men. Before Pharisees, high priests, Pilate, and "that fox" Herod, he showed a confidence that had no trace of self-abrogation.

Mushin (Nothingness) *by Shiryu Morita*

The idea of considering humility, not in relation to other human beings, not as feeling inferior, but humility before God has an important implication for Japanese life. Traditionally *enryo* (reserve or modesty) is seen as a virtue. Confucian ethics were primarily developed to maintain the existing hierarchical society, and they emphasized the importance of acting with humility in relations with others, especially to one's superiors. It can also be safe and comforting to adopt an attitude of humility in one's personal behaviour, putting others first. In a feudalistic society avoiding being shamed and "knowing your place" were important factors in maintaining the hierarchical status quo.

Humility is a virtue, first and foremost in relation to God and before God, rather than in relation to our fellow human beings. Too often the latter is given precedent. We approach humility from the point of view of self-adjustment in horizontal relationships. Human self-centredness and self-will are very strong even in those who try to be humble. To try and counteract this one of Zen Buddhism's basic concerns is the attainment of *mushin*, (a state of mind of nothingness). This is a very important but very difficult task.

60

In the Bible the vertical dimension of humility is presented through the image of the humble servant of Christ.

"Do nothing from selfishness or conceit, but in humility count others better than yourselves. Let each of you look not only to his own interests, but also to the interests of others. Have this mind among yourselves, which you have in Christ Jesus, who, though he was in the form of God, did not count equality with God a thing to be grasped, but emptied himself, taking the form of a servant, being born in the likeness of men. And being found in human form he humbled himself and became obedient unto death, even death on a cross. Therefore God has highly exalted him and bestowed on him the name which is above every name, that at the name of Jesus every knee should bow, in heaven and on earth and under the earth, and every tongue confess that Jesus Christ is Lord, to the glory of God the Father" (Phil. 2:3-11).

This appears to be a brief confession of faith of the early Christian community. The image of Christ given here is not of a hierarchical God but of a suffering servant, obedient unto death, even death on a cross. There are three important points in the passage. First, as we have learned, humility here is based on Christ's humility before God, obedience to God rather than to other human beings.

Secondly, Christ's humility is characterized in terms of "emptying himself, taking the form of a servant, being born in the likeness of men. And he humbled himself and became obedient unto death, even death on a cross" (Phil. 2:7–8). This is the key passage of what we call kenotic Christology which has a deep meaning today, in relation both to dialogue with people of other faiths and to the Christian presence in an increasingly secular world.

Thirdly, the passage illustrates the notion of Christocentric humanism. The key term is the Greek verb *kenoo*, which means to empty or deny. Christ, who pre-existed in the form of God, had to empty himself to be born as a human being. Many of us wish to practise humanism, but it is an elusive goal. Humanism has been advocated repeatedly throughout history. We see it in the Renaissance, the Enlightenment and the modern and post-modern periods. We make an effort to promote humanism through the application of reason, power and morals, but we learn that sadly we are frequently unequal to the task.

In today's world there are a number of reasons for this, for example the ambivalent and ambiguous views held by individuals and societies, and the emphasis placed on free market economics and the freedom of individuals. There is a growing gap between the rich and the poor. There is widespread frustration and isolation as individuals and communities become aware of their inability to counter huge social and economic forces. Our world is an increasingly dehumanized one, not only because of collective oppression in its many forms, but aided also by the process of social Darwinism – "survival of the fittest" – which appears to relate as strongly to the human species as Darwin's original theory does the rest of the natural world.

Some who make such a critical assessment of this world, attempt to direct their attention in an other-worldly direction (such as the attainment of *nirvana*) and withdraw from life. Some fanatical sects claim that the catastrophic end of history will leave behind all human misery. Through the Bible we see an alternative – here when Jesus Christ, God, became human he was not a man trying to escape from human misery, nor was he a man trying to be God. Because God became human in Christ we all have a basis to be human. This is what is known as christocentric humanism. It is based on the idea that Christ emptied himself in order to take the form of servant and be born in the likeness of man. And he was obedient unto death, even death on a cross (Phil. 2:8).

In the 17th century, kenotic christology (self-emptiness) was advocated by the Lutherans. At holy communion, they received the bread and wine – representing the self-emptying act of Christ. In the 19th century, it was looked for in the historical evidence. More recently kenotic christology has again received attention, from such leading theologians as Karl Barth and Dietrich Bonhoeffer as the basis of human formation and presence in the world.

In continuing with this theme, Rinzo Shiina (1911–73) is another important figure to have made a significant contribution to modern Japanese literature as a Christian novelist. In comparison with Shusako Endo (see Chapter 4) who was a second-generation Christian (Roman Catholic) – because of his mother's faith, Shiina was a first-generation Christian and a Protestant. Endo studied abroad, and is widely known both in Japan and further afield, Shiina is less known, not only because of his difficult style of writing but also because of the complex existential motifs which run throughout his writing.

The main theme in his novel, *Beautiful Women*, is the freedom accomplished in spite of the threat of death. Shiina was born in a small village outside of Himeji, to the west of Kobe. His real name was Noboru Otubo. He left home without completing high school and took a series of menial jobs, such as fruit shop worker, apprentice cook and delivery boy at a restaurant. In 1929, he became an assistant to a conductor in a private railway company in the western part of Japan. Believing in workers' solidarity, he joined the labour union of the railway company and worked hard to improve working conditions. He did not know that the union was under communist control.

In 1931, he was arrested under the maintenance of public order act, established in 1925 primarily to outlaw communist activities. He received a sentence of four years' imprisonment. He left prison in 1933 with a stay of execution for five years. In prison he was badly tortured and very nearly died. Through the experience of being confronted with the power of death, he started a journey to search for hope and the will to live. In prison he read a Japanese translation of Nietzsche's *Ecce Homo*, in which Nietzsche talks about death as a giant man. Although not convinced by Nietzsche's augments he became interested in the name of Jesus, whom Nietzsche often criticizes.

He started to read the Bible after being introduced to it by a Christian minister whom he met while participating in a peace meeting. So from communism, through Nietzsche and Dostoevsky, Shiina made a true spiritual journey and finally encountered Jesus of Nazareth. He was baptized in 1950. One of the reasons he became a Christian was the hope he found in Jesus who took the form of humanity and brought freedom from death through the cross and resurrection. His favourite portion of scripture was the scene of Christ after the resurrection as he was walking with his disciples on the road to Emmaus, sharing their conversation, and taking a meal together (Luke 24:13–35). Shiina took the resurrection so seriously that the pastor from whom he received his baptism later came to take the historical Jesus seriously; Shiina then left his church and transferred his membership to another church that confessed Christ as the Risen Lord.

After the story of Emmaus, Jesus appeared among the disciples and said:

> Why are you troubled, and why do questionings arise in your hearts? See my hands and my feet, that it is myself: handle me, and see, for a spirit has not flesh and bones as you see that I have. (Luke 24:38–40)

Shiina pays special attention to the fact Jesus not only shows his hands and feet but allows others to touch them. Shiina says, "They must have seen and touched Jesus' hairy legs. This is very humourous!"

Then the scripture continues to describe the scene as follows:

> And while they still disbelieved for joy, and wondered, he said to them, "Have you anything here to eat?" They gave him a piece of broiled fish, and he took it and ate before them. (24:41–43)

Shiina believes this scene of Jesus with his hairy legs eating broiled fish with his disciples is somewhat humorous. It reflects the reality of the resurrection, the relaxed freedom understood as the freedom from death.

After his baptism Shiina wrote a great number of novels and essays that reflected his Christian faith. Perhaps the most important work is a novel entitled *Utsukushii Onna* (*Beautiful Woman*) (1955), in which we find the central figure expressing an outlook of hope and humour even in the midst of the somewhat grey and depressing reality of ordinary life. The novel is suffused with humour stemming from his Christian faith, according to which nothing is absolute, even death is relative, conquered as it is by the cross and the resurrection of Jesus Christ.

Shiina Rinzo holds a very significant place in Japanese literature. This is partly due to his unusual experience of converting from communism to Christianity, but also due to his social and existential concerns about despair and death. Hope and despair are in fact one of the central themes of modern Japanese literature. Although Soseki Natsume (1867–1916) did not commit suicide, the central figure of his major work, *Kokoro* (1914) did.

Ryunosuke Akutagawa (1892–1927), perhaps the most brilliant writer in the history of modern Japanese literature, read the Bible with appreciation yet ended his life by committing suicide. Similarly Osamu Dazai (1909–48) in the post-war period made an existential search for a way out of the bondage of despair and death. He also read the Bible and came very close to Christian faith but also committed suicide. Aware of the struggle of Shiina's life, many critics predicted that he would be the next to commit suicide. In this sense Shiina is a vitally important writer: out of his existential experience of agony and anxiety, he made a decisive turn to find a life of hope secured on the cross and resurrection of Jesus Christ.

Sound the Bamboo

CCA Hymnal 2000

Sound the Bamboo, *Hymnal of Christian Conference of Asia*

Epilogue:
Sound the Bamboo

Sound the Bamboo is the title of the new hymnal of the Christian Conference of Asia. It was originally published in 1990 and revised in 2000. In publishing this hymnal, the editors indicated their reason for using bamboo in the title: "Bamboo groves have always been part of the Asian landscape. They appear as recurring motifs in the poetry and painting of the region. Both useful and beautiful, they suggest to the human mind the very essence of peace and harmony with nature, specially as they respond to the breeze." Furthermore, it is interesting to note that the editors express even the symbolic nature of the hymnal through the image of bamboo flute: "Bamboo flutes are ideal for people on a journey. This new CCA hymnal likewise is intended to encourage Asian Christians on pilgrimage into God's future."

Coming Home on the Ox's Back, *woodblock print by Tomikichiro Tokuriki*

The image of bamboo flutes fits in the Asian setting, especially since it reminds one of the tradition of ox-herding. After searching for and finally catching the ox, one rides on

Bamboo path

the back of the ox to return home. One no longer needs a tight rope to control the ox, instead a bamboo flute and soft music are all that is needed.

Our earthly journey is a temporal one. It seeks to arrive at the eternal city. We know how fragile we are and that we stumble along the way. Yet we proceed on our journey with hope in spite of wind and snow, just as bamboo springs back again and again after being bent by the storm. We continue our journey, renewing ourselves, just as the bamboo root – a symbol of regeneration and rebirth.

As we travel we certainly all enjoy the clean wind as it comes through the bamboo grove. It brings an air of refreshment to the weary traveller and invites us to reflect on the work of the Holy Spirit, who guides us and sustains our journey. We are citizens of the heavenly city (Phil. 3:20) and we are strangers and exiles on earth (Heb. 11:13).

On this road we meet with men and women, Christians and those of other faiths and other ideologies, as well as those who hold no particular religion. We face common issues and work under the same weather. On this road we are involved in dialogues based on hope. In this we

The Road to Emmaus *by Tadao Tanaka*

can recognize the bamboo stem, which shows emptiness, not our self-emptiness, but Christ's emptying himself, taking the form of servant, being born in the likeness of humanity and becoming obedient unto death on a cross (Phil. 2:7–8).

We know that we are not travelling alone. As on the road to Emmaus, he is with us, entering into conversation and joining our common meal (Luke 24:13–35).

Reading List

Masao Takenaka, *God Is Rice: Asian Culture and Christian Faith,* Geneva, WCC, 1986.

Masao Takenaka and Ron O'Grady, *The Bible Through Asian Eyes*, Auckland, Pace Publishing, 1991.

Masao Takenaka and Megumi Yoshida, *Consider the Flowers – Meditation in Ikebana,* Tokyo, Kyo Bun Kwan, 1990.

Wilfred Cantwell Smith, *Toward A World Theology*, Philadelphia PA, Westminster Press, 1981.

H. Richard Niebuhr, *Christ and Culture*, New York, Harper & Brothers, 1951.

Daisetsu Suzuki, *Zen and Japanese Culture*, Princeton, Princeton UP, 1970.

Acknowledgments

WCC Publications and the author, Masao Takenanka, would like to thank the following who have kindly given permission to reproduce their work in this book. WCC Publications has made all efforts to obtain permission to use the following illustrations, and apologizes for any oversights.

Bamboo grove, Kyoto, Japan, Yuriko Kurose.

Preface
Clean Wind Gradually Comes, Masao Takenaka; Bamboo fence, Yuriko Kurose; stamps depicting bamboo from China, Singapore, Korea and Japan, Yuriko Kurose.

Chapter 1
Tea house, Kobe College, Japan, Yuriko Kurose; Bamboo fence, Kyoto, Yuriko Kurose; Bamboo fountain, Kansai Seminar House, Kyoto, Masao Takenaka; Bamboo sandals, Kyoto, Yuriko Kurose; People *Taking Refuge in a Bamboo Thicket*, Hiroshima Panels Foundation, Iri and Toshi Maruki; Noh theatre, Kansai Seminar House, Kyoto, Masao Takenaka; *Winter Plum Blossom*, Masao Takenaka; Neeshima family seal, Doshisha archives.

Chapter 2
Modern Madonna, Sadao Watanabe; Dambanang Kawayan (Fishermen's Chapel), Manila, the Philippines, Masao Takenaka; *Madonna of Bamboo*, Carlos V. Francisco; *Pista sa Nayon (Bamboo Dance)*, Carlos V. Francisco; *Jesus and Children*, Luke Chen; *Holy Mother and Son*, Mali and Wo Ye; *Bamboo Rooted in the Rock*, Bao Guping; Cross and Maria-Kannon engraved on bamboo, Ikenaga Collection, Kobe City Museum, Japan; *Two Maria-Kannons*, Sadao Watanabe.

Chapter 3
Reflection on Bamboo, Yuriko Kurose; *Bamboo*, Cheng Hang Kyo; *Clean Joint and Common Root*, Mokugetsu.

72

Chapter 4
Bamboo beside the Rock, Mokugetsu; *Bamboo*, Abbot Sadayasu; *Bamboo, Clean Wind Ever Fresh*, Mokugetsu; *Two Friends in a Bamboo Grove*, Mokugetsu; Tea whisk, Yuriko Kurose; Pure Heart Tea House, Kansai Seminar House, Kyoto, Masao Takenaka; *Bamboo beside the Rocks*, Nezu Museum, Tokyo; Maitreya *bodhisattva*, Eikando Temple, Kyoto; bronze *fumie* tablet, Sawada Miki Museum, Oiso; *Darkness and Wisdom*, Yoko Magoshi.

Chapter 5
Bamboo stem, Yuriko Kurose; Diagram of a bamboo root, Hata Okamura; *Root vegetable*, Mokugetsu; *Mushin (Nothingness)*, Shiryu Morita

Epilogue
Sound the Bamboo, Christian Conference of Asia Hymnal 2000; *Coming Home on the Ox's Back*, Tomikichiro Tokurki; Bamboo path, Yuriko Kurose; *The Road to Emmaus*, Tadao Tanaka.